HOW TO MAKE AN EFFECTIVE SPEECH

OR

Presentation

DONALD H. WEISS

amacom

AMERICAN MANAGEMENT ASSOCIATION

This book is available at a special
discount when ordered in bulk quantities.
For information, contact Special Sales Department,
AMACOM, a division of
American Management Association,
135 West 50th Street, New York, NY 10020.

Library of Congress Cataloging-in-Publication Data

Weiss, Donald H., 1936–
    How to make an effective speech or presentation.

    (The Successful office skills series)
    Includes index.
    1. Public speaking.   I. Title.   II. Series.
PN4121.W3478   1987   808.5'1   86-47826
ISBN 0-8144-7672-4

Printing number

10 9 8 7 6 5 4 3 2 1

CONTENTS

Introduction
Managing the Butterflies

"Make a speech? Me? I'd rather die first. *I mean it.*"

Nothing frightens most people more than having to stand up in front of a group and deliver a speech. Butterflies infest the stomachs of even some of the greatest performers. Bob Hope, Carol Burnett, Liza Minnelli—all of them have been known to struggle to walk out on the stage.

How about you? Do you suffer from stage fright or something akin to it? If so, pay attention.

Making a speech doesn't differ that much from ordinary talking. In fact, as you'll see by reading on, in some ways making a speech is easier than making small talk.

At one time, perhaps, only a relative handful of people regularly made speeches or presentations. Today, a growing number of people find themselves center stage by virtue of their job or their position in the community or their membership in some type of professional or social organization: sales presentations, reports to their managers, reports to the committee or community representatives.

And most people count themselves in the same boat as the hero in my case study—Henry Suarez, a 28-year-old personnel administrator in a city government deep in the heart of Texas. Until he received his promotion into this position, Henry had escaped the ordeal of standing in front of a group of people of any kind and making a speech. Then, with his very first assignment from Shirley Evans, director of personnel, Henry found himself *on stage*. He was asked to present the department's human resources study to the city council during its summer budget hearings—no simple task even for an experienced orator.

And given his background, Henry qualified as something less than an experienced orator. He had enlisted in the air force immediately after graduation from high school. After spending most of his four-year tour as a medical orderly in a psychiatric ward, he returned to school on the G. I. Bill.

To earn his B.A. in psychology and complete a number of hours toward an M.A., he had barely passed English comp and had gotten through school on term papers graded *for content only.* Never once did he have to make an in-class presentation, and having little interest in school activities, he made no speeches to the general student body. Henry was just like most people— not an orator and scared to death of being one.

Henry's position with the city had been his first full-time job since graduation, and for three years, he pretty well hid himself from public attention as a personnel assistant. His promotion ended his anonymity. The presentation, because it addressed several sensitive issues, not the least of which was spending public money during a tight economy, would thrust him under the spotlights.

His job, as Shirley explained it to him, was to conduct research on current needs, make a five-year projection, prepare the documentation, and deliver the staff position. He would then summarize and print his research data on a fact sheet and human resources budget request. These being the only written materials he would give the city council before or during the meeting, he had to flesh out the proposal with his oral presentation. They would record the session live and transcribe it for distribution to the council members before their annual retreat in August. Since it was only one part of the department's total presentation, Shirley would help him, and she would introduce the subject and him to the council.

Henry's presentation could influence the city's human resources appropriation for the next five years. All this came at a time when the city government experienced the same loss of federal funds and the same budget crunch as almost all other municipalities—and during an election year in which most city council members promised, "No new taxes." How's that for a scary way to enter the world of speechifying?

Well, Henry did it. And he shined. Most of all, what he lacked at first was the same self-confidence everyone afraid of speech making lacks. You gain that self-confidence by:

1. Having a *plan* for putting together your speech or presentation.
2. *Practicing* your delivery.
3. Having the *chance to do it successfully* at least once.

A few butterflies survive up to the bitter end, but they're manageable.

By the time you've finished reading this book, you'll be in a better position to deliver your own talk. You'll see that making a presentation or a speech differs only in structure and format from holding an ordinary conversation, and you'll learn how to organize, structure, and prepare a talk—complete with audio and/or visual aids.

Chapter 1

Conversation versus Making a Speech

Though in the beginning Henry lacked the confidence to talk before a large audience, he wasn't timid or shy, and he had a fairly good gift of gab. His boss, Shirley, had confidence in him.

A little speech of her own gave him some of the confidence he needed:

> *Henry, it's a whole lot easier than you think. I've heard you telling war stories or defending some point of psychology or some piece of EEO legislation—or just talking about your family. You string words together in an interesting, sometimes very amusing, way. Your reasoning's sound, and you have a natural sense of logic and order. Anyone who can tell a story can make a speech, and you're a good storyteller.*

Henry still had his doubts. Like most people, he conversed for the pure joy of social interaction. Sure. You probably know people who take over any conversation for use as a platform to promote themselves or what they believe. Yet in reality, few people use ordinary conversation for this purpose. In fact, ordinary discourse is usually an inefficient way to get across a viewpoint.

You can promote your thoughts on a specific topic much more efficiently through a presentation or a speech. (I'll use the words synonymously to eliminate the awkward phrase.) It's actually easier to communicate this way than through a garden-variety chat.

A presentation is always *goal-directed,* whereas a chat is unguided and undirected. Since goals control the direction of the talk, and you, the speech maker, set the goals, you control the flow of the discussion. You can make it two-way if you wish, but in the main, your speech will be a one-way communication—from you to your audience.

Just look at the opportunities you have when you make a speech:

1. *The opportunity to talk to (sometimes with) other people about something of interest to them, which meets their needs as you perceive them.*
2. *The opportunity to bring your opinion or point of view to the attention of other people through goal-directed, well-developed, well-rehearsed, usually uninterrupted talking (with or without audio or visual aids).*

You can never do in an ordinary conversation what you can do when making a speech that you plan in great detail, coordinate with audio and/or visual aids, rehearse, and fully control.

Chapter 2

Planning a Speech

Broad planning for a speech consists of defining its general topic and your goal for making it. You then move on to a more detailed level of planning, in which you establish the structure of your presentation and how you will make your points.

Goals and Topics

Effective planning before making a speech gives you a sense of security. You know what you're going to present, how you're going to do it, and why you're doing it in the first place.

Henry had been handed an unenviable mandate: persuade the city council to accept the staff proposal for a five-year human resources plan. The general *topic* was the personnel needs of the city for the next five years. His *goal* was persuasion. As you can see, there's a big difference between a topic and a goal.

Though Shirley handed him *both* his topic and his goal, most times you're only asked to discuss a topic; the goal of the talk you decide. The topic answers the question, "What am I talking about?" The goal answers, "Why am I making this talk? What outcome do I want?" The topic responds to an *interest;* the goal responds to a *need*.

The city's elected representatives had an obvious interest in its human resources requirements. However, to the staff, it seemed the council members didn't understand the level of personnel needed to perform the services that the citizens demanded (or that the staff thought they demanded). Shirley and Henry rightly designed their goals to meet the *needs* of their audience *as they perceived them,* even though their audience didn't see those needs at the outset.

Think about the great stars' stomach butterflies. They get them from anxiety—fear that their material won't go over with their audience, fear that their writers didn't perceive the needs of the audience correctly. Yet they go out there and give it their all because, after years of success, they figure, "Well, we haven't been too far off up till now, so I guess we'll hit the mark again."

When you think you know what your audience needs, you can set a goal that meets those needs. The goal you set determines the kind of presentation you make. Knowing that you're heading in the right direction with this audience boosts your confidence.

Having a goal gives you a point of view, without which your presentation falls flat. It gives you confidence because while the topic establishes *what* you're talking about, the goal establishes *why.* It gives you a reason, and having a reason for doing something makes doing it seem right.

You design your goals to meet the needs of the audience as you perceive them, whether or not the audience sees those needs at the outset. Your job is then to get them to confirm your perception or to finally agree with it.

Structuring Your Talk

Goals give direction and style to your presentation. Structure makes the presentation effective.

Deciding in advance how you're going to structure your speech, especially how you'll present your facts and draw conclusions from them, will build your confidence to deliver it. When you realize you've got a good grasp of your content and a sound method for making your case, you feel much better about what you're doing.

As with writing effectively, a talk has to have an outline. It not only tells the audience where you're going and how you're going to get there, it also keeps you on track. Simplistically, a presentation has a beginning, middle, and end.

The beginning. Most books on public speaking tell you to start a talk with a funny story or a joke. Well, in many cases you should, but more than anything else, your *outline* should start with a *thesis.*

When you plan, consider the beginning as the most important part of your talk. The thesis summarizes the whole thing. It also contains your point of view. Henry's thesis:

> *The city must increase its human resources this coming budget year and each year for the next five years because . . .*

The topic: human resources.

The point of view: We must increase human resources.

The summary of the talk: everything after the word *because.*

Without that statement, Henry could meander all over Texas. In essence, the thesis tells your audience what you're going to tell them.

Though it's first in your outline, the thesis needn't be the first thing out of your mouth. Instead, you can tell that funny story or joke, if it's appropriate. It'll catch your audience's attention, it'll warm them up to you, put them at ease, relax them. And you don't have to make up your own. Every library and bookstore offers books of anecdotes, jokes, funny stories from which you can select an appropriate icebreaker.

I've said the magic word twice: *appropriate.* Whether you make up the funny story or quote from another source, let your thesis be your guide. Make 'em laugh, make 'em laugh often, if that's right for your audience. Laughter's that spoonful of sugar that helps the medicine go down, as an old song says. But make 'em laugh in context. Make 'em laugh at something that moves your speech forward and, ultimately, leads them toward the thesis of your talk.

Now once the joke is over, you *rivet* their attention with your thesis. Whether your subject is heavy or light, important or trivial, the thesis on which you build your talk focuses your listeners on what you're saying and calls attention to your most important points and to what you want them to remember. And remember they will.

(When speakers lose their audience early on, you know they're not using this approach. Both they and their audience suffer through the whole performance. Sadly, those people, afraid to go through that agony again, give speech making a bad rap.)

After you've told them that you want them to remember something—your thesis—you have to give them something to remember. That's what you do during the middle of the talk.

The middle. In the central portion of your presentation, you develop your point of view. Here's where you break out each of the points of the summary after the word *because.*

Let's say that after *because,* Henry had listed four main points: without an increase in human resources, (1) basic city services would have to be curtailed, (2) taxpayers would lose the return on their money, (3) federal matching funds would be lost, (4) voters would revolt. If you look at the sample outline in the accompanying sidebar, you'll find that each of those main points in the thesis follows a roman numeral and becomes a separate topic in the middle of the presentation. Now Henry has something on which to elaborate.

Sample Outline

Thesis: The city has to increase its human resources this coming budget year and each year for the next five years because if we don't, we will have to curtail basic city services, taxpayers would lose the return on their money, federal matching funds would be lost, and voters would revolt.

I. All departments are understaffed.
   A. Studies show that a 25 percent increase is needed this year.
   B. Studies also show that a 5 percent increase is needed each year for the next five years.
      1. In-migration is increasing.
      2. Birthrate is steady, but mortality rate is decreasing.
II. We will have to curtail basic city services.
   A. Studies show that no department is able to keep up with the demand for its services.
      1. Streets and highways department is now nearly one year behind in repairing roads and building new ones.
      2. Human services department has had to subcontract for such programs as visiting nurse.

3. Water department cannot service new subdivisions.
B. No new services can be added to city government.

III. Taxpayers would lose the return on their money.
A. Taxes and bonds are investments.
B. Taxpayers are not getting the services in which they are investing.

IV. Federal matching funds would be lost.
A. Unless services are brought up to federal standards, those moneys would be held up for undetermined periods of time.
B. Competition for federal money is keener than ever; only those cities that have demonstrated past performance will get it.

V. Voters will revolt.
A. Services will have to be curtailed in your voting districts.
B. Dissatisfied citizens will not get services to which they are entitled.
C. We will experience many of the problems of other urban communities.
D. We will experience some of the social disturbances seen in the sixties.
E. The voters will scapegoat someone.

Of course, it's great when you're addressing the converted, those who already agree with you, but sometimes, as in Henry's case, you have to persuade the audience that what you're telling them is in their best interest to believe or to act upon. Either way, you develop your presentation to meet those needs. There are three basic ways of doing this: You explain something or describe something (an *exposition*); you tell a story (a

narrative); or you persuade someone to believe something or do something (*rhetoric*).

Henry had to inform and to persuade at the same time. He also felt that a story or two could help him prove his thesis. His next planning step, therefore, was to decide how to integrate all three forms into the middle of his presentation: exposition, narrative, and rhetoric.

Expository format. If you set a goal of explaining or describing something, you can mold your speech in either of two ways, which are not mutually exclusive: exposition and narrative. Henry had to use exposition, that was for sure, because *the expository form tells people what something is or how to do something.*

Using exposition, he could explain his findings to the city council. He could explain that the human resources situation in the city falls short of the city's needs. He could also explain that during the next five years, because of the rapid growth in population and demand for services, the shortfall will increase by a geometric rather than arithmetic progression. He could also explain how to prevent the personnel shortfall and the shortages that would mean.

Narrative format. But with an issue of this nature, exposition by itself doesn't really *tell the story* of the city's human resources needs. *Numbers* of new population to accommodate, *numbers* of streets to repair, *numbers* of miles of new sewer pipe to lay—*numbers,* they're all just *numbers.* Necessary but impersonal. By themselves, they don't sell budget requests.

Narrative makes a presentation personal. *A narrative describes happenings or tells a story.* Consider a travelogue. Through which would you rather sit: fifty 35 mm slide photos of the Matter-

horn or the same fifty slides accompanied by a traveler's hair-raising stories of the harrowing experiences he or she had while climbing it? Narrative makes a travelogue interesting, brings it to life.

When you must persuade, narrative adds punch to the exposition's point of view. That's why Henry needed vivid stories about people—individual private citizens affected by the lack of services that the personnel shortfall has created. Though the thesis of an exposition carries with it a point of view (its goal), it often takes a narrative to drive the thesis home. This is where Henry's skill as a storyteller came in handy.

Shirley handed him his topic—the human resources situation in the city. She gave him his goal—persuade the city council to accept their recommendations. He had to plan how he would transmit the information and how he would persuade the politicians, themselves all masters of persuasion.

Exposition and narrative would *inform* his audience of conditions, materially and substantively. But that wouldn't be enough. Narrative would help, but he needed that extra something to move his listeners to action. For this, he finally decided, he had to present a *logical case for action,* but he also had to *appeal to the emotions of the city council members before they would take action.* He would, in short, have to use rhetoric.

Rhetoric. Strictly speaking, rhetoric includes *any* effective speaking or writing. In modern usage, *rhetoric implies an attempt to persuade through writing or speaking.*

Consider that travelogue again. It doesn't seem as if you're trying to persuade anybody when you're delivering a talk about your vacation.

Still, you want your audience to think that you enjoyed the trip and that if they went, they'd enjoy it, too. Otherwise, why make the talk? To show off pictures? (I know, you've asked that of friends with slides many times.)

To win his case, Henry had to use both forms of rhetoric: the *appeal to reason* and the *appeal to emotion.*

Appealing to reason. After completing the research, Henry would have the data for appealing to reason and the narratives from which he could pull his appeals to emotion. Organization and logic ensured that, in the process of persuading his audience, he would make his appeals *sound.* His arguments made sense and couldn't be picked apart on their lack of merit. It wasn't the time to be hoisted by his own petard.

The appeal to reason takes two forms: deductive and inductive. In basic deductive reasoning, you *assume,* for the sake of argument, that what you're saying is factually true. In inductive reasoning, you attempt to show that your conclusions are factually true, that they have a high *probability* of being true.

Here's an example of a typical deductive argument. Notice the hypothetical form of its premises and its conclusion: "If [something is true], then [something else is true as well]." Notice also that the two premises below share a common clause: "the city cannot provide many of its basic services." This argument is *valid,* though its factual truth depends on other factors.

> If human resources shortages continue, then the city cannot provide many of its basic services.
> If the city cannot provide many of its basic services, then many of its citizens will not receive a return on their tax dollars.

Therefore, if human resources shortages continue, many of the city's citizens will not receive a return on their tax dollars.

Of course, Henry couldn't hope that everyone on the city council would simply *assume* that everything he said was true. City council members are hardly naive. To make his *deductive* arguments hold together, to make them *sound* as well as valid, he had to show that he could back up his assertions with evidence. He had to present *inductive arguments*—conclusions drawn from empirical data. He had to show, for example, that the city did have a personnel shortage.

Let's say it takes four people on a crew to repair a broken sewer main. Let's also say that the most the supervisors can place on a crew at any one time is three people. If that sort of situation repeats itself in a *significant number of different departments,* then it's safe to say that the city has a human resources shortage. To draw a probable inductive conclusion, *you need data sufficient enough to support your conclusion.*

Combining his deductive with his inductive reasoning, Henry came up with this sound argument:

If the city has human resources shortages, we will have to curtail services to your voting districts.

From the data, the city has human resources shortages.

Therefore, we will have to curtail services to your voting districts.

Henry made a sound case with his last argument; it was factually true and valid at the same time. But by referring to the voting districts, he went beyond logic. He knew what most salespeople know: Facts and logic alone rarely convince people to do anything. He needed to punch a button, raise some emotional issue with which the council members could relate, and they certainly could relate to curtailing services in their voting districts during an election year.

Appealing to emotions. Most of the time, to persuade your audience to accept your position or do what you suggest, you need to appeal to their emotions. That's another kind of rhetoric.

Salespeople will tell you that most people act out of emotion, not on the basis of facts or logic; people buy what they *want* more frequently than what they *need.* In a sales presentation, they describe features, but they sell benefits, something about buying their products or services that satisfies some sort of desire on the part of the customers—for example, resulting from vanity. That's what keeps high-priced boutiques in business.

So it is, too, when it comes to agreeing to something or accepting another person's point of view. There are bona fide appeals to emotion. For example, "If we don't get this dioxin cleaned up, our children will die." Or, "If you continue to use drugs, you can injure your brain or damage chromosomes." Both examples present facts, but they do so in the context of *fear tactics*—an appeal to emotion.

You can appeal to other emotions, too, as advertisers well know. "For *chic,* buy dresses by Carklein." "*Real men* use chocolate-scented after-shave." "For the vacation *of your life,* fly the Golden Bird with the big tail."

But be careful with emotional appeals. Used in the wrong contexts—contexts in which only the facts are wanted, needed, or required (for example, at a scientific meeting)—they can destroy your speech. The more transparent appeals will ruin the talk no matter what the context. You endanger yourself whenever you avoid the truth or weight of the evidence, or distort the significance of evidence, or substitute an appeal to emotions for facts or evidence.

A logic teacher's old story illustrates the misuse of these fallacious appeals. When Clarence Darrow's young partner found himself on the losing end of a trial, the wise old man supposedly said, "When all seems lost, abuse the other fellow's attorney."

The sidebar on the abuse of rhetorics lists some common violations of the rules of deductive logic and some common fallacies about and misuses of emotional appeals. You may want to look over that material before going on with the main text.

You probably have guessed by now that bona fide appeals to emotion work very well when integrated with narratives. In fact, the main purpose of using narratives is to appeal to something more than "just the facts, ma'am." Combined with a strong emotional appeal, they're facts with a kayo punch.

Personal preference dictates how you put together the middle of your presentation. All your decisions depend upon how you perceive your audience's needs and what goal or combination of goals you set for yourself.

In the middle, you weave together your goals—to tell and to persuade—through exposition, narrative, and rhetoric. The art of speech making consists of pulling all those elements together smoothly in an interesting, persuasive manner *in each separate element of the speech*.

You use facts to show that the subject matter of

The Abuses of Rhetoric

Deductive Fallacies

Equivocation: Changing the meaning or connotation of a word.

Ambiguity: Leaving the meaning of a word or phrase unclear when it can be interpreted in at least two different ways.

Vagueness: Leaving the meaning of a word or phrase unclear when it can cover a multitude of possibilities, as in *democracy, efficiency, progress.*

Begging the question: Presenting an argument in which one of the statements offered as evidence assumes the conclusion to be proved (also called arguing in a circle).

Contradiction: Asserting two statements at the same time that cannot both be true at the same time and in the same way.

Fallacies of Inductive Reasoning

Over-simplification: Attempting to support a conclusion with evidence that is too limited or one-sided, especially if the presentation of evidence is highly selective, ignoring contrary data (also called stacking the deck).

False cause: Drawing hasty conclusions about antecedent events or correlations.

| *False analogy:* | Suggesting that because two different situations or things resemble each other in some respects, they do so in most if not all other respects, as well. |

Fallacies of Emotional Appeals

Appealing to pity:	Replacing facts or evidence with an appeal for sympathy.
Appealing to the people:	Invoking traditional values, attitudes, prejudices, or provincial interests. ("As our forefathers said . . .")
Jumping on the bandwagon:	Appealing to the usual human desire to be like or do what others are like or do. ("You have to act now, because every city in the state except ours has sufficient human resources to run their services.")
Appealing to laughter:	Replacing evidence or data with satire, parody, jokes, or diversions. ("Go ahead. Don't increase our personnel. Make my day.")
Arguing against the person:	Replacing evidence or data with attacks against your opponent(s). ("The councilman doesn't want to increase human resources because he's from a predominantly white district and is therefore against Equal Employment Opportunity.")

your thesis is true. For this you use *exposition.* Henry used the statistical results of his survey, those numbers on top of numbers concerning services that were already suffering and that would suffer even more in the future. He illustrated those cold, impersonal numbers with *narratives* of people experiencing the loss of services. He explained what his projections meant with respect to decreasing levels of service and increasing individual suffering.

You tie those facts together through *rhetoric,* using inductive and deductive reasoning to support your point of view and to persuade through the use of logic. You've already seen some of the arguments Henry used. He wove that type of reasoning all through the talk. And he also appealed to emotions all along the way.

He moved from one section of his talk to another until, finally, he arrived at his ultimate goal: the end.

The end. Every speech comes to an end. Better to plan that end before you start. The end is the conclusion you've drawn and/or the summary of the position you've taken. In a real sense, the end is a restatement of your thesis, and in that sense, your closing is in the beginning.

If you've been telling a story, or a series of stories as Henry did, then you build toward your conclusion. You wait until the end, or just before the end, of your talk to reach the climax of your narrative. The climax is a forceful moment of emotion, suspense, or tension in which you reveal or reinforce the point you've been trying to make.

You know what a climax is. In a murder mystery, the masterfully brilliant detective reveals the name of the murderer. You knew that the crime was committed and some details about how it was done. Now, in the climax, you find out who and why.

In a speech, the climax usually occurs at the end. At the same time, in an effective speech, just as in a cliff-hanging thriller, you don't reach the climax in a straight line from the beginning to the end. You need to keep your audience tuned in to what you're saying by leading them through a series of little climaxes, each one of which renews interest and generates a desire to hear more.

Henry filled his speech with little stories, each of them illustrating his thesis and four principal topics: a story about potholes destroying tires and shock absorbers, a story about storm sewer lines backing up in rainstorms, a story about an old woman not receiving home health services and dying. Important stories, yet none of them telling enough of the city's story to make it complete in itself. Each contributed to a larger story that made sense only when he pulled all of the little ones together:

> And when we curtail enough of the city's basic services, this is what we can expect: a loss of citizen confidence in their government and a voters' revolt.

To drive home that conclusion, he described their city in the future—a city in which bond issues failed, in which strikes left refuse piled high in the streets, in which transportation would grind to a halt. He told the story of several modern cities, using Philadelphia and Detroit, in 1986, as two such examples.

Many first-time speakers don't know when to stop talking, just as many inexperienced salespeople go on with their presentation past the point where the customer's ready to buy, and they lose their sale from talking too much.

Not Henry. He ended at the end. He restated his thesis in a slightly different manner and left his audience with the picture he painted for them. To say anything more would have been anticlimactic.

The tell 'em principle. I can best summarize this business of outlining with the tell 'em principle:

Tell 'em what you're going to tell 'em. Tell 'em. Tell 'em what you've told 'em.

People remember best what they hear at the beginning and end of a speech. Summarize the talk at both ends and the audience will retain a good portion of the stuffing when they leave.

Chapter 3

Watch Your Language!

Plan what you intend to do with your presentation, structure the presentation, marshall your facts, and build your arguments—then use language that lulls everyone to sleep, zooms over their heads, or speaks down to them. You've wasted all your other effort.

How do you prevent that? KISS 'em—the KISS principle. That's an acronym for "*Keep it simple and straightforward.*" (Yes, I know. You've probably heard it as "Keep it simple, stupid." Well, I don't think you're stupid; otherwise, you wouldn't be reading this book.)

You keep what you say simple and straightforward through the words you choose and how you string them together. Your high school English teachers called it *diction.* They weren't referring to how you pronounce your words. They meant choosing the right words to express what you mean. And *your choices should depend on the nature of your audience,* no matter how literate you may think you are.

Use ordinary, everyday language, *except* when presenting to an audience of experts on your topic. Then, make sure you're using their jargon or buzzwords correctly. Avoid slang if you think your audience may be offended by it.

At the same time, don't be afraid to make your language interesting. Tickle your listeners' imaginations and stretch their intellects with colorful action verbs rather than static verbs such as *to be, to do, to have.* Let *nouns* describe your topic and issues rather than strings of adjectives or adverbs. Though economy of language brings home your point more forcefully than does wordiness, punch up your presentation with similes, analogies, and metaphors; they give your talk some pizzazz.

Similes, analogies, and metaphors capture your audience's attention fully. On the other hand, blow obscure or obtuse figures of speech by them, and you'll lose them entirely.

Similes, analogies, and metaphors all make comparisons between people, things, or happenings, differing from one another only in fullness and form. Whereas an analogy usually makes a rather full comparison, showing or implying any number of points of similarity, a simile pinpoints a comparison, pointing the way with an introductory word—*like* or *as*. Of the three, a metaphor makes the shortest or most compact comparison; it implies rather than points out the likeness between the things compared by claiming that one thing *is* another in some respect.

Analogies help you communicate or emphasize ideas or describe situations to people who know very little about your topic. Tie together several points of similarity, instead of just one, between what you're saying and the audience's experience. You stand a better chance of making yourself clear that way. Henry used the following analogy in his speech to the council:

Would you deprive this growing city of its human resources any more than business-people would deprive their business of the personnel that make the firm productive? Businesspeople hire the personnel they need to keep their business productive, to make them enough money to hire more people to produce and sell more goods and make more money. We need enough people to do the city's business—the business of providing the services that will attract more people and businesses to thrive in this city and to buy the city's services.

Henry also used similes, which differ from analogies insofar as they identify just one similarity in their comparisons. Your everyday language is loaded with them—*red as a rose, hungry as a horse, off like a shot.* Those similes are clichés, of course, but you can fill your talk with more inventive ones if you wish to make your figures of speech accurate, clear, and interesting. Look at one of Henry's:

Reducing city personnel is like driving a car without insurance. We may get away with it for a few months or even a year, but sooner or later, we'll be caught short without the help we need in an emergency or crisis. In the end, it's false economy.

Metaphors make the most compact comparisons, also of just one similarity, but they usually make a talk most colorful or interesting. That's why poets and other lyric writers fill their pages with them. Henry ended his presentation with one that left his audience with a very sobering thought:

Without the people it must have to serve the needs of our citizens, this city will become an enfeebled phoenix, unable to rise from the ashes of the fire we ourselves have set.

A stirring figure of speech, that. A forceful appeal to emotion. But what if the council members hadn't known what a phoenix is? Or that the mythical phoenix is supposed to rise from its own ashes? What if the only Phoenix of which they knew was a city in Arizona? (And when did it burn down? Wasn't that Chicago?)

I'm exaggerating, of course (another figure of speech that can work well in a talk). Everyone knows that the phoenix was a mythical bird in ancient Egypt, represented as living for many centuries, only to arise from the ashes of the funeral pyre it set for itself, once again a youthful, fresh, and powerful creature. Everyone knows that, don't they?

You probably get my drift. Colorful language can endanger your speech if your audience doesn't understand it. If those council members didn't understand Henry's metaphor, his point would have been lost. So, it's essential that you speak to the level of your audience's understanding.

When talking to a group with whom you're unfamiliar, research who and what they are. Those star performers I mentioned earlier have advance men and women who go ahead into the next town to report on community tastes, topical issues, and touchy subjects. Confidence comes, in part, from the intelligence they get about their audience.

If you don't know the audience, ask the person who invited you to speak. You may get a slanted or biased view, but it's better than knowing nothing. Did you ever hear a speaker tell a story that seemed funny to him or her but that the listeners found off-color? Then you know what I mean.

Ditto for assaulting your audience with language you've acquired through education that they may not have had. Many Ph.D.'s with a lot to say wind up saying little that's intelligible because they know *too* much. They never learned how to communicate to people ignorant of their subject matter.

In another book in this series, *How to Write Easily and Effectively*, I tell writers to use the "grandma test." Speakers can use it, too. Practice your speech in front of someone unfamiliar with your topic—perhaps your own grandma. If he or she follows the talk with little or no difficulty, it passes your grandma test (assuming your grandmother's not a Ph.D. in your subject matter, of course). I'll have more to say about practicing your speech in a later chapter.

KISS. Keep it simple and straightforward, but make it interesting at the same time. People remember what they think is simple and straightforward. They remember if you make the simple and straightforward interesting and alive, as well.

Chapter 4

Involve Your Audience

Select appropriate goals, put the talk together in an orderly and interesting fashion, fill your speech with literate and artistic figures of speech—then read it from a prepared text, head down, eyes riveted on the print, neither paying attention to your audience nor giving them anything worthwhile to see. They'd remember you, all right, but I don't think you'd like to know how.

Plan ways to leave each person with the *feeling* that you spoke directly to or with him or her. Try for as much interaction as possible. Interaction lets people contribute to the presentation. They don't feel that you're patronizing them. And the more *they* say, the smarter they think *you* are.

Soon after you start, ask people to tell you what they want to come away with, given your topic and background. Ask as many as you can within the limits of your time and the size of your audience. Have a flipchart and marker available, if possible; list their responses; and refer to those expectations frequently, whether or not you've written them down.

After you've made a number of successful talks, you'll find it much easier to discover the topic that is of interest to the group, research that topic and the group, and then make the presentation based on the importance of the expectations you elicit from the group. You'll also find that if you've done your homework, few of their expectations will come as a surprise to you.

In the middle part of your outline, set down places at which you can point out how what you're saying fits their needs. They'll feel that you're tailoring your speech for them, and when you get good at this business, you *will* tailor your speech for your audience on the basis of the expectations they list for you.

Identify also places where in the middle you can ask *open-ended questions* of your audience. The difference between open- and closed-ended questions is important. No one can answer an open-ended question with a yes or no. Open-ended questions begin with the words *who, what, where, why, when, how.* They demand answers—descriptions, explanations, or explications. They can be one-word answers, but they have to be something other than a yes or no. Good reporters or interviewers make extensive use of them.

"What do you want for this city?" Henry might have asked that good question. "Who do you expect will fill those potholes?" would really have sparked a good debate. He would have gotten nowhere if he had asked, "Do you want to fill those potholes yourselves?" Or, "Are you going to appropriate more money for human resources?" City council members could have answered both questions with a no, and he would have gained little in the way of audience involvement.

You don't always have to ask questions to get people talking, contributing ideas, information, or feelings. "What do you think?" can be converted into "I know you have some good ideas" followed by a pregnant silence. Nature abhors a vacuum, and silence is a sort of vacuum.

Many speakers, when teaching people how to do something, use a special form of interaction that allows the learners to assimilate the lessons very quickly. In jargon, it's called *experiential learning.* In everyday English, a close equivalent is *practice.* Let people learn by doing.

Confucius, history reports, said:

Tell me, and I hear.
Show me, and I see.
Let me do, and I understand.

Talking *at* people reduces learning to 25 percent. Show and tell increases learning to approximately 50 percent. Showing, telling, and letting them do raises retention to over 75 percent—and it's fun, too.

If you're teaching people *what* a piece of machinery can do, plan to show a film or a videotape of the machine in action. But if you're teaching them *how to operate* that machine, plan to make it available. Tell them about it, show them how to do it, then let them touch it, manipulate it, and run it themselves. Otherwise, they'll only *know about* it, or at best, they'll *know something about* how to operate it, but they *won't* be able to operate it themselves.

If you're teaching interpersonal-relations skills—say, conflict resolution—design activities that will let your audience experience what you're teaching. They can practice the skills on each other. The simplest way, especially if time is short, is through a *fishbowl exercise.* Have two or more people come before the whole group to work through a simulation of the skill you're teaching. Have the group discuss the interaction they watched, giving feedback to the players and to one another in the process.

Poorly managed fishbowls can blow up. The audience could poke fun at the players or chide one of them for something, causing everyone to retreat from the interaction in your presentation. It's more effective to set up small-team activities, dividing the group into units of from two to four people to go through some activity, such as a role play or a short discussion.

Finally, prepare some way of getting feedback from your audience after your talk ends. You can ask, either on a printed form or just by going around the room: "What specific information or feeling did you get from this talk? How did the talk meet your needs or expectations?" You need this information from them as much as they need the opportunity to tell you.

Planning how you'll involve people gives you the confidence to let them become involved, and they'll feel that they, too, have a stake in the success of your talk.

Chapter 5

Using Visual and Audiovisual Aids

Whether or not you use interaction, to give your talk a touch of class, add visuals or audiovisual aids. They run the gamut from simple flipchart pages prepared in advance to a multimedia show. It all depends upon your creative imagination, your time for preparation, and your resources.

Show and tell works especially well when you're talking about relatively complicated matters or otherwise dull factual data. As I said earlier, people remember as much as twice the information you provide when you *show* them things as well as talk about them.

Videotape or film constitutes the best material for aiding a talk. Conditioned to a video format, people respond well to action-oriented moving images that illustrate what you're saying. If you don't have the videotape or film that best illustrates, demonstrates, or emphasizes your main ideas, you can rent one and the equipment to show it (or have your hosts rent them). Many libraries catalog educational and/or training and motivational films, from which you can select one that meets your needs.

If you can't get your hands on a motion picture or video to show, there are alternatives. Opaque projectors can be used to project such items as pages from books. Thirty-five mm slides can be very effective; so can transparencies shown on an overhead projector. If you have a 35 mm camera, or if you have a flair for making either slides or transparencies, create your own. Otherwise, buy or rent what you need from an educational supply house or a processing lab that can create computer-generated slides.

Take a look at Figure 1. Called a storyboard, it's a way of coordinating your slides or transparencies with your text. To create a storyboard, sketch in a drawing of your slide images or write out your verbal message. Be sure to use images that illustrate your point. The storyboard serves as your outline for the presentation.

Caution: If you use words on your slides, keep

Figure 1. Storyboard: Human Resources
Report

Photo: large potholes in surface of a major highway.	*The city's major arteries already suffer from unrepaired potholes. If we continue to deny the streets and highways department the additional personnel it requires, the problems will get worse for drivers.*
Photo: new car with broken front axle.	*Damage to automobiles is only one of the consequences of severe street damage.*
Split screen: two-car collision (left), pothole (right) with cars in background.	*Serious accidents result because drivers lose control of their cars, whether or not the cars are damaged by the potholes.*

them to a minimum. Printed words on a screen tend to be dull and to distract. If you can't say it in ten words, don't say it at all.

It's best not to leave any one image on the screen for too long. Pacing depends on how many slides you have and how they're connected to the text. The length of one paragraph should be long enough. If you don't have an immediately following slide turn off the projector rather than leave an image up for too long. Again, it will bore and distract the audience.

If you have the resources, mix sound and still

pictures. You can mix audiocassette tapes and slides through electronic impulses (audible or silent) that advance the slides to keep pace with the words. Many professionally made audiovisual programs are available for rent also, with catalogs in many libraries.

Do you have access to extraordinary resources? Then dazzle 'em with a multimedia show: multiple projectors mixed with audiotape in one part of the presentation, video materials in another, transparencies or flipcharts—all woven together into an interesting mosaic of sight and sound that rivets audience attention. On the other hand, *too much* of a good thing can overwhelm and detract from your message, and it's your message that counts.

Regardless of how simple or how sophisticated your AV's, don't lose sight of your audience's needs and your goal. Make sure that anything you put in front of those assembled fits both.

Chapter 6

Rehearsing Your Presentation

How many times, after a conversation, have you wished you could take back your words ("If only I hadn't said that") or wished you had said something you should have ("Why didn't I tell him what I really thought?")? Oh, Lord. Life's one long sequence of missed opportunities.

Behold one of the great advantages of making

a speech! If you're not an expert on the topic you're assigned, you can research it thoroughly; you can become, hopefully, more of an expert than the people in your audience. You can pull all your random notes together; develop your outline, choosing your language and your arguments with great care; practice your speech and *rewrite* anything you *shouldn't* have said or *insert* something you *should* have. *You're in control.* Any missed opportunities are your own fault.

Research your topic. Even if you're an expert, bone up on the finer points of what you intend to say. Make sure you have sufficient information to make your talk thorough and interesting, and enough evidence to back up whatever persuasive positions you take.

Another caution: Don't substitute study for getting the job done. Research sometimes becomes a rationalization for procrastination, and the next thing you know, the date of your speech crashes down around your head.

Generate your ideas first as random notes. Let them flow freely onto an idea sheet. Don't even worry at this time about misspellings. Use the idea sheet in the sidebar as a model. It's Henry's idea sheet for the portion of his slide presentation dealing with the human resources shortage in the streets and highways department. Look it over now before continuing.

Idea Sheet

potholes
streets and highways dept
Not enuff people to fill the holes before the next
    freeze makes new ones
Pictures—lots of photos of potholes, accidents

The Loop—has to be the worst road in town
Synchronize tape
Do it live, advance with remote.
Loss of fed funds if we don't repair properly
Can't repair the roads fast enuff
Department down by 25%
Need to increase by 25% this year and by 5%
   each year just to keep pace, not get ahead of
   problem.

Sift through those random thoughts for ideas to pull together as your thesis or main points and your point of view. That's the tool you need for editing the random thoughts, first by eliminating redundancies, repetitions, and irrelevancies. That's what Henry did with his notes.

Rewrite the notes into a topic outline or, if you're an experienced writer, into a sentence outline. You may want to leave a topic outline as is. Sometimes you need only cue words—key concepts, issues, or points—to use as notes for making your talk. Other times, you may want a sentence outline to ensure that you state your important points exactly the way you want the audience to hear them.

Still another caution: Avoid writing out your talk word for word. You could too easily succumb to the temptation to *read* it rather than deliver it.

Practice as much as possible. Memorize the speech if you can. Practice early enough in front of a friendly someone; get feedback you can use for revising the speech and practice it some more. Then, before the actual presentation, make a dry run—a dress rehearsal with all the AV's, as well.

Have your dress rehearsal in front of an audience. Round up a few colleagues from the office and have them play critics. Fine-tune the talk using the feedback you get. The success of your talk derives, in part, from the fact that the feedback comes from *an audience,* even if it isn't *the* audience for which the speech is prepared.

Well, that's it for the planning. You've researched your topic, you've formed your point of view, you've put everything together just the way you want it, you've rehearsed it and rehearsed it. Now, the moment of truth is upon you. Time to deliver your speech, and *how* you deliver it will test the value of the work you put into it.

Chapter 7

Making the Speech

Expect lingering butterflies. Everyone has them. It's a form of stress, your body and mind's mobilization of energy for doing what has to be done. Worry, but don't let your anxiety overwhelm you. Remember that you're prepared, well prepared. You know more about the subject than the people to whom you're speaking (or at least, as much as they do). Concentrate now on how you deliver your speech.

Maintain your presence or poise. Speak to one person at a time, making eye contact with everyone you can. Generate a commitment and an enthusiasm for your topic and point of view, communicating them with appropriate animation and gestures. Move about. Pace your delivery, modulating your pitch and volume. Deliver your talk rather than read it. Introduce your AV's. Interact but maintain control.

Most people who feel they can't make a public presentation simply forget that they do many things in public all the time—cheer at ball games, walk hand in hand with a sweetheart or spouse, comment out loud in movie houses. More important, they ignore the fact that they talk with people constantly. Standing in front of a group of people frightens them because they see the assembled body as a large number of people rather than as a collection of *individuals* to whom they can speak one at a time.

Start by thanking the person who introduced you, lest you offend him or her. Thank the throng assembled for giving you the opportunity to speak. If you know other people in the room or hall, acknowledge as many of them individually as you can. They'll become allies and boosters, if you need them.

Let everyone think you're talking specifically to or with him or her—especially if you're urging the group to believe or do something—by speaking to your audience, not only to their level of understanding but also literally to each person. Make eye contact with every person you can, as far back into the room as you can. Turn your head, your whole body if possible, from one side to another (at reasonable intervals, of course). Not only does each person feel immediately in touch with you, you feel immediately in touch with one person at a time.

If at all possible, don't tie yourself to a lectern, but when you move, make it deliberate and purposeful. Place a visual aid a few feet away, go to it as you talk about it, then return toward your audience. Avoid quick movements or pacing back and forth rapidly. You'll communicate nervousness and lack of self-confidence to your audience and distract them.

Along with tone of voice, gestures—facial and hand—communicate what you feel about the subject. Emphasize your points by raising your eyebrows, smiling, moving your hands appropriately. Avoid jabbing motions, such as pointing a finger at someone. They threaten and accuse. (Of course, you may *want* to threaten or accuse someone; then, such gestures are appropriate.)

Time your movements and gestures to the pace of the talk. Pacing makes all the difference in the world. Too quick a delivery and no one picks up on your key points. Too slow a delivery and everyone goes to sleep. Pause at the end of a major point to let it register, but don't hold the pause too long, lest you let your audience's mind wander off.

Watch your audience for reactions. Facial expressions and body language tell you whether you're on target. And respond to those reactions.

Let's say several people seem puzzled. They're frowning or appear to be on the verge of asking their neighbor or you for additional explanation. Don't pick on any one person, but say something like, "I want to be sure I'm making myself clear." Then look straight at someone who seems puzzled. "I'd like a question or comment from the audience on that." He or she is likely to respond.

If that person doesn't, find someone else and repeat the invitation. "It's important to me that I not go on unless I'm sure we're all on the same wavelength."

Coordinate your pitch and volume with your main points, movements, and gestures. If you're making an important emotional pitch, don't deadpan it. If you're making an important factual presentation, don't overload the talk with heavy emotion.

Here's a cute device for holding attention, but for only a short time. Lower your pitch and volume at the same time; force people to strain a little to hear you. Then suddenly raise both pitch and volume to drive home your message.

Earlier I said to memorize your speech if you can. If you have to use a script, try not to read from it, losing contact with your audience. No one's interested in the bald spot on the top of your head or in the way your hair is permed. Your audience came to see your face as well as hear your voice. Let them.

If you can't memorize your material, use note cards with a topic outline on them. Use very large print or type on note cards or in a full-length script; it helps you follow your talk and maintain your place throughout. If you can obtain a teleprompter, use it.

If you're using visuals or audiovisual aids, introduce them early in the talk. Explain their purpose and their content. Just before you use them, explain why you're doing it. Then, afterward, summarize what they showed or said. Henry introduced the slides for his streets and highways department segment this way:

> *To show you just how serious this matter is, I've prepared a series of visual aids. Even better than the numbers, they demonstrate how great the need is. . . .*

He summarized the slide show with:

> *Now that you've seen those slides, you'll realize that this one department alone can cripple the ability of this city government to effectively protect its citizens from damage to life, limb, and property.*

When showing visuals, keep some picky but important points in mind. Don't come between the light source and the screen. Your shadow interests no one. Don't turn your back on your audience to talk about an image you've projected behind you or to the side. Look at the transparency or stand at the side of the room to talk about the image, especially if it's a 35 mm slide. And don't stand in the back of the room unless no other arrangement is possible or unless you do it for some dramatic effect.

Finally, interact but don't lose control. Some people may try to take control from you. Hear them out, but keep control by summarizing their remarks and going on with what you have to say. They feel acknowledged, even though they've lost the struggle they began with you.

Henry didn't engage in the little dialog below. I made it up, but it could have happened, and if it had, here's how Henry could have handled it:

Mayor: Much of what you're saying, I've said before. This council has heard me say repeatedly that unless we recognize the importance of our citizens' needs and meet them, they'll vote us out of office. Isn't that what you're saying, Mr. Suarez?

Henry: You're saying that our citizens' needs have to be met, and I agree. What I'm saying, moreover, is that unless we increase our levels of personnel, we cannot meet those needs, and . . .

By not answering the mayor's closed-ended question with a simple yes or no, Henry did four things: (1) He acknowledged the mayor's point of view; (2) he agreed with one critical point in the mayor's little speech; (3) he used it to build his case further; (4) he retook the floor. That's control.

Another way to maintain your focus is to redirect. Choose someone else to comment on a long-winded person's remark. That takes the power away from the first speaker and transfers it to someone else—at your discretion.

Henry: That's an interesting point of view, Mr. Mayor. How do the rest of you feel about that?

Of course, while that question would redirect attention away from the mayor, it also jeopardizes Henry's control. If no one had spoken up in answer to that open-ended question he had asked of everyone in general and no one in particular, the *awkward* silence in this instance could have made him look foolish.

If no one speaks up, pick someone from the group to answer. "Mr. Jones, you've been on the city council longest. How do you feel about it?" "Madam, what do you think of what the mayor just said?" Direct your questions, if you have to, and acknowledge the answers.

You can acknowledge an answer merely by a "That's very interesting." Or you can make the acknowledgement more extensive: "I'm glad you brought up that subject. The way I see it . . ." It's O.K. to discuss an opinion, but avoid debating with your audience. Even if you win, you lose.

People want respect from their speakers as much as the speakers want the respect of their audiences. Teach yourself to refrain from debating an answer to a question you ask. A debate is the quickest way to lose your audience's respect. Acknowledge the answer, acknowledge your disagreement, and then acknowledge the right of the other person to hold that opinion. Chances are you'll win him or her over in the end.

Here's another dialog I made up to illustrate the point. Remember Henry's metaphor of the enfeebled phoenix? What if the mayor had taken exception to it?

Mayor: Mr. Suarez, I think you're exaggerating with that business about the phoenix and fire and ashes and stuff.

Henry: In what way, Mr. Mayor?

Mayor: The citizens of this city are a little more civilized than you give them credit for.

Henry: If I understand you, Mr. Mayor, you think the citizens would never get tired of having their needs frustrated by inadequate services, that we could never have a Watts or a Detroit or a Newark here.

Mayor: That's right. Do you think that could happen here?

Henry: At this moment, yes, sir. It doesn't mean you're wrong. You and I may be seeing the situation from two different perspectives. I'd like to know more about yours. Maybe we can find areas in which we agree and from which we can develop a plan that would meet both points of view.

In that exchange, instead of debating with the mayor, Henry offered to work with him to build a plan out of their differences of opinion. A less resourceful and rational person might have said simply: "Mr. Mayor, I've got the facts right here. You don't know what you're talking about." That person wouldn't hang around city hall long enough to hear the mayor's well-chosen 5,000 epithets.

In the accompanying sidebar, you'll find a summary list of all the dos and don'ts of this chapter. Study them well and take them seriously. Your butterflies will all disappear when you hear the ovation you get upon finishing.

Dos and Don'ts of Delivering a Speech

Do	*Don't*
Use appropriate humor, especially to open the talk.	Tell jokes or stories that are likely to offend.
Thank the host or hostess.	Forget the host or hostess's name.
Thank the group for the opportunity to speak.	Ignore people in the group whom you know.
Find out the group's expectations.	Wander off your topic.
Stick to your topic and goal.	Be inflexible if the group's needs for you differ from your expectations.
Use as many visual aids as you think necessary.	Overload visually.
Maintain rapport with the audience.	Use wordy slides or transparencies.
Make eye contact with as many people as possible.	Distance yourself with stilted or arcane language.
Memorize your speech if at all possible.	Read from your notes or a script.
Use appropriate inflections and tones of voice.	Speak in a monotone or too slowly.
Use appropriate gestures and movements.	Speak too quickly, in too high a pitch, or too loudly or softly.
	Ignore audience reactions.

Keep control through directed interactions.	Argue or debate.
	Lose control to long-winded people.
Introduce and summarize AV's.	Try to answer questions for which you don't know the answers.
Summarize your talk.	
Thank your audience again.	Stand between the light source and the screen.

Conclusion

A Speech Is a Most Efficient Way of Talking

I honestly believe that anyone can stand up in front of a group and make a speech—anyone who can talk or otherwise communicate. If you're honest with yourself, you know you can. You've done it many times.

That's right. You may say you've never done it, but think about the number of times with family or friends or co-workers that you held forth on some subject or declaimed some strongly held opinion—your child's first tooth, your mother-in-law's last visit, the boss's tendency to give you something to do at five minutes to five on Friday afternoon. Never? I doubt that.

How many times at a party have you complained mightily about the number of months a year you're working for the federal, state, and local governments? Did you not debate with people the merit—or lack of merit—of some of the politicians running in the last election? C'mon, admit it. You make speeches all the time, don't you?

Most people do. The security in making these kinds of speeches comes from the familiarity you have with the audience you managed to trap. At the same time, if only you'll take that same public presence you display in those circumstances and carry it into a slightly different environment, you'll see that you're just as good at expressing yourself in a more formal setting as you are in the intimacy of your social circle.

Most people, when called upon to make a formal presentation or a speech, panic. They convince themselves they can't do it. As a result, they don't do it well. And that's a shame because frequently they have something worthwhile to say, something that becomes lost in disorganization; in *hems, haws, ers;* in an overly fast delivery or one that's too slow or too dull.

They don't realize that inside every successful public speaker there exists a nervous person for whom making a presentation or a speech is little more than talking to or with other people. Anyone who can hold a conversation can become a *public speaker.* All they need to gain the confidence that kills butterflies are organization and practice.

A speech is a more efficient way of communicating your ideas than is unrehearsed or informal chitchat. It's a goal-directed, planned, and rehearsed opportunity for speaking your mind to or with people who have asked you to hold forth. They want you to talk with them, to tell them your opinion on some subject of interest to them. You get a chance to talk about something that meets their needs, whether they perceive their own needs or not. How often do you get a chance like that during an ordinary, everyday conversation?

Though you're usually asked to speak on a specific topic, you almost always get to choose the goal of your talk: to inform or to persuade. They're not mutually exclusive. Effective speakers weave the two goals together, ultimately convincing the listeners to agree with them or at least acknowledge the possible truth of their position.

Not only does having a goal give you confidence, a well-planned outline supports you as effectively as a cast supports a broken leg. It tells your audience where you're going and how you're going to get there. Like a book, a speech has a beginning, middle, and end.

The beginning contains your thesis, in which you state your topic and your point of view. It's the "Tell 'em what you're going to tell 'em" part of your talk.

The middle is where you tell 'em. You tell them through exposition, narrative, or rhetoric, or through some skillful interweaving of the three. You state the facts, as you see them. You describe situations that illustrate the facts, and you champion your cause through logic or appeals to emotion. And that brings you right up to the end.

In the end, you tell 'em what you've told 'em. You take them to the climax of your talk either by drawing a conclusion that influences the listeners in some way or by summarizing what you've said so that it all comes together. Of course, you can do both. (If you look closely at this last section of the book, you'll see that I'm doing the same thing here.)

When you put together your presentation, keep it simple and straightforward. KISS 'em. Use language everyone understands, but make it interesting: colorful action verbs, descriptive nouns, analogies, similes, and metaphors. Let the assembled body *see* what you mean.

If necessary to help them see, use visual aids. Back up your words with pictures of some kind. Give your presentation visual punch.

Get involved with your audience. Interact with them by at least asking them questions or letting them ask you questions. Make them partners in your presentation, and they'll take some of the responsibility for making the speech successful. Just don't lose control of the speech. Use the dos and don'ts in the previous chapter.

That's it. Everything you ever wanted to know about how to make a speech in public. Efficient, and it's as simple as it looks.

INDEX

ABOUT THE AUTHOR

Donald H. Weiss, Ph.D., of Millers' Mutual Insurance in Alton, Illinois, has been engaged in education and training for over 26 years and has written numerous articles, books, audio cassette/workbook programs, and video training films on effective sales and supervisory or management skills. He speaks regularly on stress management and other personal development subjects, and has produced a variety of related printed or recorded materials.

During his career, Dr. Weiss has been the Manager of Special Projects for a training and development firm, the Manager of Management Training for an insurance company, the Director of Training for an employment agency group, a training consultant, and a writer-producer-director of video training tapes. He also has taught at several universities and colleges in Texas, including the University of Texas at Arlington and Texas Christian University, in Fort Worth.

Currently, Dr. Weiss is Corporate Training Director for Millers' Mutual Insurance.